POPULAR MUSIC IN CANADA FROM THE ’60s, ’70s AND ’80s

JUDITH KLASSEN ✦ ERIN POULTON

Library and Archives Canada
Cataloguing in Publication

Title: Retro : popular music in Canada from the '60s, '70s and '80s / Judith Klassen, Erin Poulton.

Other titles: Popular music in Canada from the '60s, '70s and '80s | Popular music in Canada from the sixties, seventies and eighties

Names: Klassen, Judith, 1976- author | Poulton, Erin, author. | Canadian Museum of History, issuing body, host institution.

Series: Souvenir catalogue series ; 35.

Description: Series statement: Souvenir catalogue series ; 35 | Issued also in French under title: Rétro : la musique populaire au Canada des années 60, 70 et 80.

Identifiers: Canadiana 20250162024 | ISBN 9780660726441 (softcover)

Subjects: LCSH: Popular music—Canada—Exhibitions. | LCSH: Popular music—Canada—History and criticism. | LCGFT: Exhibition catalogs.

Classification: LCC ML3484 .K63 2025 | DDC 781.640971—dc23

Published by the
Canadian Museum of History
100 Laurier Street
Gatineau, QC K1A 0M8
historymuseum.ca

Printed and bound in Canada

Graphic design by:
InnovaCom Marketing & Communication

This work is a souvenir of an exhibition developed by the Canadian Museum of History and presented by Power Corporation of Canada.

TABLE OF CONTENTS

FOREWORD

Retro shines a spotlight on popular music in Canada from the 1960s, '70s and '80s. If you came of age in this era, you may feel a sense of nostalgia as you leaf through this book — recalling an outdoor festival, a dark underground club, or turning up the volume on your radio to hear a favourite song. But the vibrancy of this music isn't confined to the era in which it was written — it continues to reverberate.

The shared experience of enjoying popular music transcends generations, and yet each person's relationship with this music remains unique and personal. In this way, *Retro* is more than a look back. It's a short journey through an important cultural moment — a time when popular music both inspired and reflected social change. Canadian artists innovated and collaborated, in many cases influencing the sound of music worldwide. New musical forms took shape, and new voices made themselves heard. A Canadian music industry gained momentum, but not without raising critical questions about art, culture and identity that remain equally relevant today.

The singers, songwriters and musicians showcased in these pages are among those who have had a lasting impact on popular music in Canada. Many have become enduring icons internationally, and many continue to create, perform and release new music. If you listen, you can hear the echo of their influence resonating in the work of new artists today.

James Whitham

Vice-President, Research, Collections and Exhibitions
Canadian Museum of History

Music Is Culture

Popular music exploded in Canada during the '60s, '70s and '80s.

Popular music is not a single style or genre, and goes far beyond the Top 40. It is something we listen to, move to, and identify with. It transports us to different times and places. It is social, personal and political — sometimes all at once.

Popular music doesn't just reflect culture. It **is** culture.

This book is about creativity, self-expression, subversion, and play. It showcases popular music in Canada during three formative decades, exploring how musicians, listeners and communities forged new paths, created new spaces, and developed new forms of expression. The music of this era is explosive in its energy, and its reverberations continue to impact the cultural spheres that we inhabit today.

Retro also examines how popular music was interwoven with the social and political happenings of the time. From Willie Dunn's poetic lament in "I Pity the Country," to the intimacy of Joni Mitchell's *Blue* album, to metal bands like Voïvod that upended conformity, popular music shapes — and is shaped by — moments, movements, and social realities.

There is no single popular music narrative in Canada. *Retro* brings together many stories — and storied objects — from a wide variety of artists and moments. Through this diversity, we can begin to experience the energy of this dynamic period.

CHAPTER 1

POPULAR MUSIC IS...

SOCIAL

Artists and listeners collaborate and experiment. They create shared experiences and build communities. Popular music brings people together.

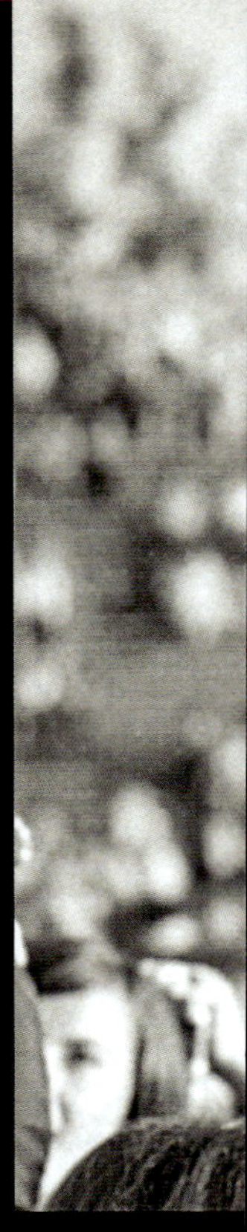

Toronto Rock 'n' Roll

Canadian Bandstand
CKCO-TV in Waterloo, Ontario
Around 1969

Youthquake

CANADA WAS PART OF AN INTERNATIONAL POP EXPLOSION IN THE EARLY 1960s.

As the first baby boomers moved into their teens, they became a powerful new audience. Radio, live concerts, and music programming on television helped shape an emerging youth culture. International audiences embraced many of the same bands, and Canada was part of the action.

The Power of Radio

RADIO DJs AND MUSIC DIRECTORS SHAPED THE TASTES OF A YOUNGER GENERATION.

As portable radios gained popularity, more listeners could choose their own stations. Programming no longer needed to target the whole family, and teens became a specific new market. In 1957, Toronto's CHUM 1050 became the first station in Canada to adopt a "top hits" format. Many other stations would follow suit in the 1960s.

Music on Television

IN THE 1960s, MUSIC-THEMED PROGRAMS BROUGHT ARTISTS FROM ACROSS CANADA RIGHT INTO FAMILIES' LIVING ROOMS.

Shows such as *Music Hop* and *Jeunesse d'aujourd'hui*, which featured Canadian bands playing the hits of the day, created a sense of connection among youth. The sets were bold, and the atmosphere was high-energy. Eager fans took part in live tapings.

Michèle Richard

Michèle Richard rose to fame in the 1960s. This Quebec music and style icon projected a modern image that appealed to young audiences.

Her popularity reflected Quebec's strong and growing celebrity culture, which included music-centred television shows, magazines, and newspapers, as well as a popular-music awards system.

Michèle Richard's "Miss Radio-Télévision" Award
1967

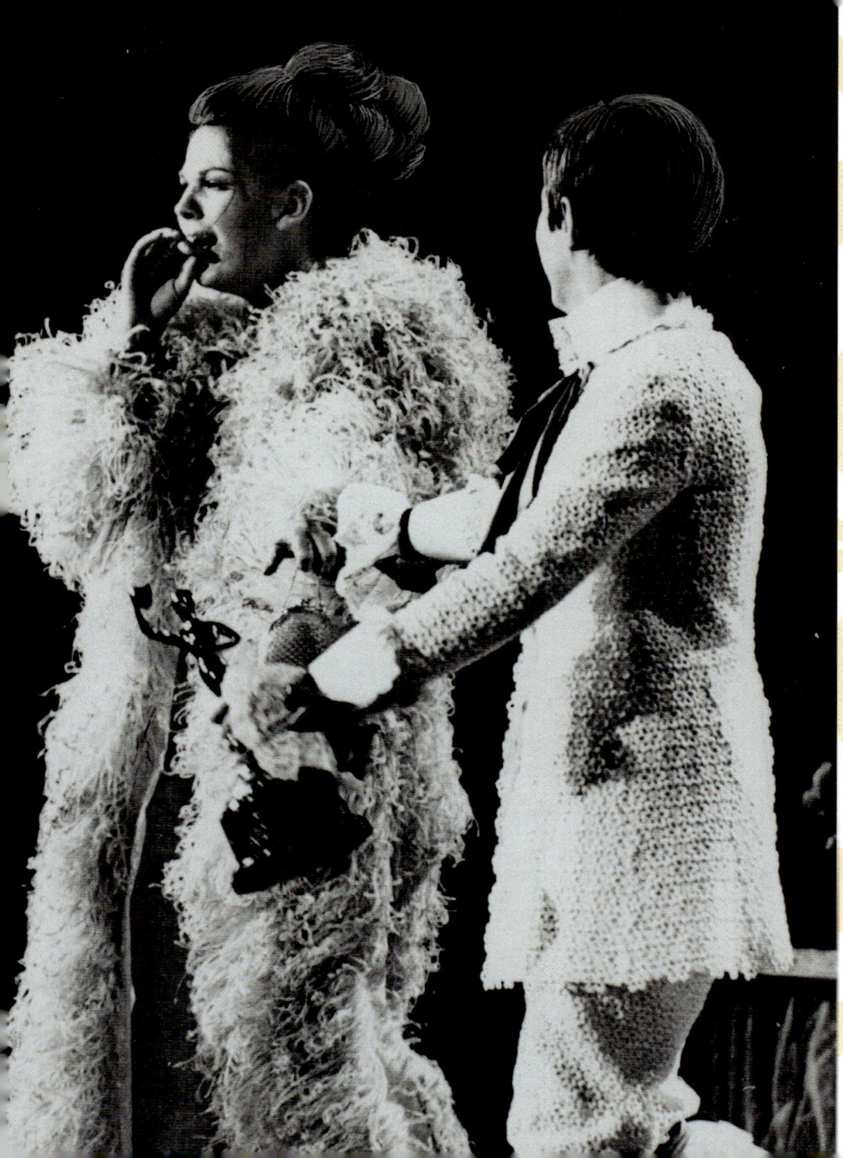

Michèle Richard is named "Miss Radio-Télévision"

May 29, 1967

Yéyé: A French Phenomenon

YÉYÉ WAS EXTREMELY POPULAR IN QUEBEC AND FRANCE. IN QUEBEC ALONE, THERE WERE MORE THAN 500 *YÉYÉ* BANDS DURING THE 1960s.

With their unique looks and energetic performances, *yéyé* artists were a fixture on French-language music television shows. They performed both original songs and translated versions of well-known English hits. Attracting young fans, *yéyé* artists helped to spark a francophone fan culture and star system in Quebec.

Stage clothing worn by the lead singer of César et les Romains, Denis "Dino" L'Espérance

Around 1965

César et les Romains

In the early 1960s, Dino et les Questions formed in Rouyn-Noranda. The group became César et les Romains in 1965, gaining attention with their playful onstage look, which included Roman tunics and gladiator sandals. César et les Romains captured the youthful nature of *yéyé*, covering songs such as Bobby Darin's "Splish Splash" and The Beatles' "Yesterday."

Innovation and Inspiration

CANADIAN ARTISTS WERE INSPIRED BY THE EXPLODING YOUTH CULTURE OF THE 1960s.

↑ Left to right: Neil Young, Bill Edmondson, Jeff Wuckert and Ken Koblun
September 1964

Many Canadians enjoyed British Invasion acts like The Beatles and The Rolling Stones. French pop stars, such as Johnny Hallyday and Sylvie Vartan, were also popular among francophone youth. Canadian artists were influenced by these musicians' styles and sounds, while also expressing their own individuality.

Neil Young and The Squires

Although its members were still in high school, The Squires gained a large local following in the early 1960s. They performed at community centres, church halls, high schools, and music clubs around Winnipeg. The Squires played cover songs, but also performed original music, including the two rock tracks on their only recorded single.

The tracks on The Squires' 45 RPM single are Neil Young's earliest recordings as a songwriter and performer. Roughly 300 copies were pressed — fewer than 15 are known to remain.

Left to right: Trevor Dailey, Everton Pablo Paul, Terry Lewis, Jay Douglas, Newton Barker and Gary Gabriel

Rouyn-Noranda, Quebec
1969

Jay Douglas and The Cougars

Jay Douglas came to Canada from the West Indies in 1963. The Jamaican Canadian artist soon became lead singer of The Cougars, a dynamic Toronto R&B band. The Cougars navigated Toronto's conservative music scene, gaining attention through their electrifying live performances. They had a regular gig at the now-legendary Le Coq d'Or Tavern in downtown Toronto, and toured extensively throughout Ontario and Quebec.

Jay Douglas performed in this tailor-made suit during the late 1960s and early '70s.

Left to right:
Randy Bachman, Garry Peterson, Burton Cummings and Jim Kale
Around 1966

The Guess Who

Winnipeg's Chad Allan & The Expressions released their cover of "Shakin' All Over" under the name "Guess Who?" to encourage the idea that they might be a British band in disguise. It worked — the song reached No. 1 in Canada. By 1970, The Guess Who had many original hits, including "American Woman," which topped the Billboard Hot 100 that year.

Randy Bachman crafted this "Flying V" guitar in 1965, using wood from a closet door and parts from an old Fender Telecaster.

Toronto's Caribana cruise

July 1981

Making the Scene

THERE IS A STRONG CONNECTION BETWEEN POPULAR MUSIC AND THE PLACES WHERE PEOPLE EXPERIENCE IT.

From rural community halls to downtown discos, and from intimate coffee houses to eclectic festivals, popular music in Canada has often been a shared experience. During the '60s, '70s and '80s, vibrant regional scenes and local venues created spaces where artists and fans could gather, build communities, and experiment with new sounds and experiences.

People also rebelled against authority and broke down barriers between genres and among audiences. Each scene was unique, shaped by the people, places and creativity that brought it to life.

↑

Sparkles Nightclub inside the CN Tower
Around 1979

The Disco Scene

FLASHY DISCOTHÈQUES DREW PEOPLE TOGETHER TO DANCE, EXPERIMENT, AND BE SEEN.

Montréal was the disco capital of Canada in the 1970s, with a market second only to New York in all of North America. Artists such as Toulouse and Purple Flash were known for their electric stage presence and rhythmic, highly danceable music. Discothèques were often inclusive spaces, and a beacon for 2SLGBTQIA+ and other historically marginalized communities.

Pierre Perpall

Pierre Perpall, also known as Purple Flash, is a dynamic pop, disco and dance pioneer who emerged in the 1960s. He was one of the first Black artists to appear on music television in Quebec. His hits in French and English include "J'aime danser avec toi," "We Can Make It," and "Keep Doing That Thing."

↱ Pierre Perpall commissioned this futuristic outfit for "We Can Make It."

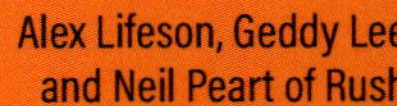

Alex Lifeson, Geddy Lee
and Neil Peart of Rush

1978

Make Some Noise

ARTISTS TOOK LIVE ARENA SHOWS TO A WHOLE NEW LEVEL IN THE 1970s AND '80s.

As concerts expanded into arenas and stadiums, large-scale immersive experiences became possible. Spectacular stage settings, light shows, and pyrotechnics captured the excess of the period, while also engaging the senses. Flamboyant stage clothing and larger-than-life performances further amplified the experience.

Alex Lifeson's
Doubleneck Electric Guitar
Gibson EDS-1275
1977

Neil Peart's Drum Head
1970s

Rush

Rush formed in 1968, in the Toronto suburb of Willowdale. The power trio went on to become one of the bestselling rock bands in history.

The members of Rush have been called the "godfathers of progressive metal." They are celebrated for their technical mastery, epic instrumental suites, and spectacular stage performances. Rush's carefully crafted lyrics explore fantasy and futuristic themes, question conformity, and champion the underdog.

↰

Geddy Lee's Doubleneck Electric Bass/Guitar
Rickenbacker 4080
1976

Diane Dufresne

Diane Dufresne is celebrated for her theatrical strength, musical sensitivity, and provocative style. With success in Quebec and France, she has been described as the first female francophone rocker.

"La Diva" has sold out stadiums, thrilling fans with her powerful vocal ability and stage presence. Her 1972 debut album, *Tiens-toé ben j'arrive!*, topped the charts for six weeks in Quebec.

Diane Dufresne
1973

Trooper

Trooper formed in the early 1970s. By the end of the decade, the Vancouver rockers were packing arenas across Canada.

They took their stage presence seriously — along with lights, the band's high-energy shows included pyrotechnics. In 1980, Trooper won the JUNO Award for Group of the Year. Many of their rock anthems, such as "Raise a Little Hell" and "Two for the Show," remain well known across Canada.

Trooper's Ra McGuire (right) and Brian Smith
September 1975

↑ Lead singer Ra McGuire's stage clothing, designed by his wife, Debbie McGuire, in the 1970s

Crusaders
NAME

New wave band Spoons signing autographs at Sam the Record Man
Toronto, Ontario
1984

Browsing the Racks

RECORD STORES WERE IMPORTANT SCENES. LISTENERS CAME TOGETHER TO DISCOVER, SHARE, AND TALK ABOUT NEW MUSIC.

Flipping through records was about more than shopping. Immersed in a space dedicated to popular music, listeners engaged with people who shared their passion and curiosity. The chance to hear new releases, and a variety of genres, gave this environment its own special energy.

Music lover Basil Philistin collected these 45 RPM singles released by Canadian artists who were big in Japan.

Canadians Break Through

THROUGH INTERNATIONAL CONNECTIONS, CANADIANS HELPED SHAPE THE SOUND OF POPULAR MUSIC.

Artists from other countries began to seek out Canadian musicians for their distinctive approaches to sound. Through this collaboration and exposure, Canadians created new sounds and innovative experiences. They also developed international fan bases with hit songs that crossed borders.

Céline Dion at Eurovision
1988

Céline Dion

Céline Dion gained international attention as a teenager in the 1980s, winning awards in Quebec, France and Japan. Her 1987 album, *Incognito*, sold 200,000 copies in Quebec alone.

In 1988, Dion won the Eurovision Song Contest as Switzerland's representative, with the song "Ne partez pas sans moi." Within two days, it had sold 200,000 copies in Europe. Soon after, her first English hit, "Where Does My Heart Beat Now," made the top five in the U.S.

Anne Murray

Born in Springhill, Nova Scotia, Anne Murray is one of Canada's most acclaimed singers. Her crossover sound — combining pop, country, and adult contemporary — has had an enormous impact, both nationally and internationally.

Murray has sold more than 55 million albums, and has received numerous awards, including more JUNO Awards than any other artist (as of 2024). She broke ground as a female artist, embracing her rural Maritime roots while forging a major international career.

↰

Anne Murray wore this hand-beaded outfit on tour in 1978. She described it as reflecting designer Juul Haalmeyer's "penchant for the flamboyant."

Anne Murray
1970s

Rick Danko and Janis Joplin on the Festival Express train
1970

Spotlight on Sounds

MUSICIANS EXPERIMENTED, COLLABORATED, AND INSPIRED ONE ANOTHER, CREATING WHOLE NEW SOUNDS.

During the 1960s, artists played with the boundaries between styles and genres as never before. They often jammed together, influencing one another with surprising results. This creative exchange continued through the 1970s and '80s.

The Band

The Band started out as The Hawks, playing back-up for Ronnie Hawkins — a dynamic performer and mentor to many Canadian artists. They also played with Bob Dylan before establishing themselves as an act in their own right.

Their work incorporated blues, folk, country and rock in songs such as "The Weight" and "Up on Cripple Creek." Somewhat ironically, although most of The Band's members were Canadian, their influential sound came to be known as "Americana."

Robbie Robertson played this 1920 Gibson Model O guitar during The Band's memorable concert film, *The Last Waltz*.

Michel Normandeau played this dulcimer with Harmonium in the 1970s.

Harmonium

Artists challenged the boundaries between genres in many ways. Some groups, such as Montréal's Harmonium, brought folk, rock, pop and jazz influences into their work. They explored rock as a serious artistic medium, experimenting with unexpected instruments.

Songs like "Depuis l'automne" capture this emerging progressive style, incorporating instruments rarely heard in rock music, such as the dulcimer, zither harp, and flute.

Harmonium co-founder Michel Normandeau with his dulcimer
1976

CHAPTER 2

POPULAR MUSIC IS... PERSONAL

Music is a unique experience for each of us. Musicians and listeners find ways to express their inner worlds through popular music.

D'Arcy Street Block Party
Toronto, Ontario
May 1971

Looking at an LP
1969

Something Personal

PEOPLE LISTEN TO AND SHARE MUSIC EVERY DAY, BUT OUR RELATIONSHIP TO MUSIC REMAINS UNIQUELY PERSONAL.

Listeners connect with songs, and use them to connect with other people. They associate certain songs with memories, experiences and relationships. Popular music is more than a personal soundtrack — it is a way of expressing emotions, individuality, and inner worlds.

Personal Technologies

IN THE ’60s, ’70s AND ’80s, SOUND TECHNOLOGIES EMPOWERED PEOPLE TO CHOOSE AND LISTEN TO MUSIC ON THEIR OWN TERMS.

Popular music became more affordable, accessible and shareable. Radios became ever smaller, making it possible to listen on the go. Budget-friendly vinyl singles also remained popular, allowing people to buy and share the latest hits. Portable cassette players combined both access and mobility, providing the ultimate personal experience.

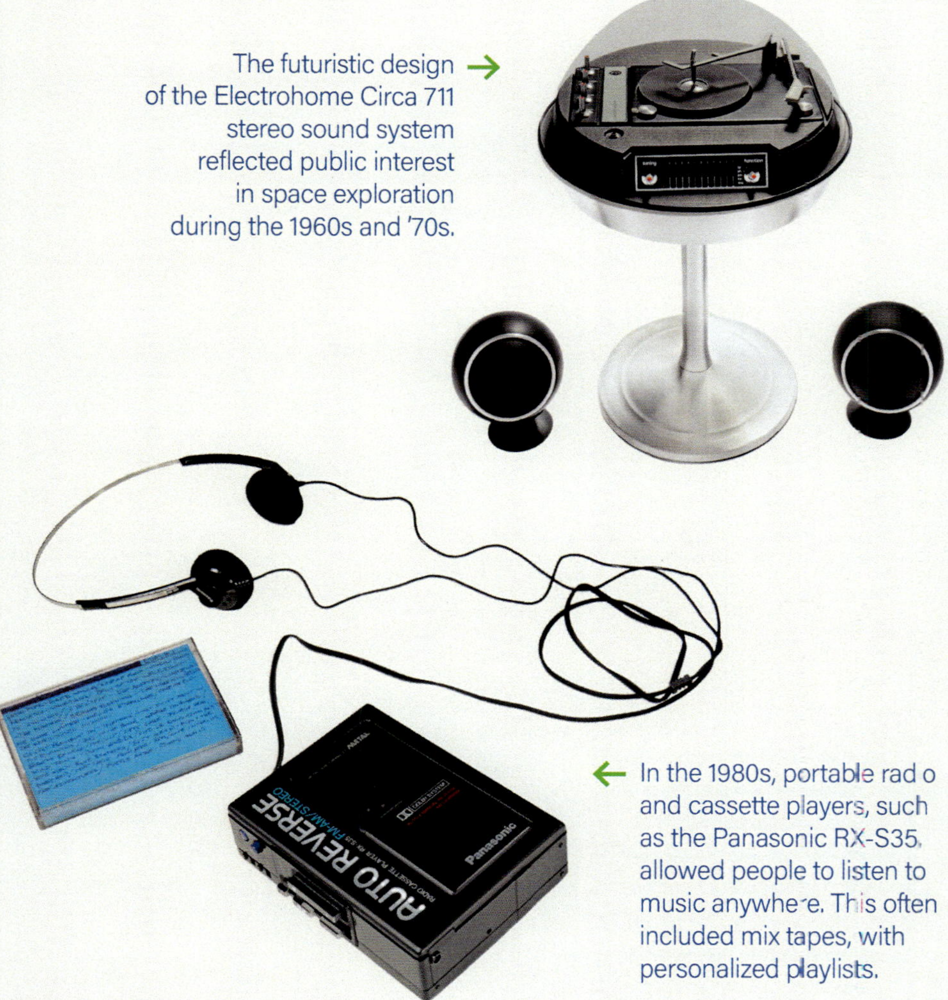

The futuristic design of the Electrohome Circa 711 stereo sound system reflected public interest in space exploration during the 1960s and '70s.

In the 1980s, portable radio and cassette players, such as the Panasonic RX-S35, allowed people to listen to music anywhere. This often included mix tapes, with personalized playlists.

Rough Trade band members, left to right: Sharon Smith, Carole Pope and Jane Cessine
April 1975
↳

Breaking the Rules

ARTISTS IN THE 1970s AND '80s FOUND NEW WAYS TO PUSH BOUNDARIES.

During the 1960s, singer-songwriters charted fresh territory through personal lyrics. Building upon this momentum, later artists expressed themselves through new forms of sound and self-presentation. They exposed the unseen, and even the taboo, to reveal their inner worlds and identities.

Carole Pope and Kevan Staples of Rough Trade in a promotional image taken by their label, True North Records

1980

Rough Trade

Innovators with close ties to Toronto's art and theatre scenes, Rough Trade addressed then-taboo themes using humour, wit and satire. "High School Confidential," for instance, was the first Top 40 hit to overtly explore lesbian desire, and band member Carole Pope often performed in bondage attire and other creative stage clothing.

Kashtin

Innu artists Claude McKenzie and Florent Vollant met on the Maliotenam reserve, located near Sept-Îles, Quebec, and began performing together as Kashtin in 1984. Songs on their 1989 self-titled album were performed in Innu-aimun, a language spoken by roughly 11,000 people.

Kashtin sold more than 200,000 albums internationally, bringing mainstream attention to music performed in an Indigenous language. Some of their best-known songs include "E Uassiuian" (My Childhood), "Tipatshimun" (Song of the Devil), and "Tshinanu" (Ourselves).

Florent Vollant and Claude McKenzie
1989

Mitsou

Mitsou's dynamic public persona evokes confidence, empowerment and playfulness. She co-wrote and co-composed many of her songs. As a teenager in 1988, she crossed the French–English musical divide with her debut album, *El Mundo*. The album went platinum, selling 100,000 copies. "Bye bye mon cowboy" became a hit in both French and English Canada — a rare feat.

← **Mitsou's "Bye bye mon cowboy" outfit incorporated clothing from her own closet.**
Around 1988

Music Meets Video

VJs at MuchMusic in Toronto. Left to right: Christopher Ward, Denise Donlon, Michael Williams and Erica Ehm.
1980s

COMBINING MUSIC WITH MOVING IMAGES, VIDEOS BECAME A POWERFUL MEDIUM FOR STORYTELLING.

Music videos soared in popularity during the 1980s. Many teens rushed home from school to watch shows such as CBC's *Video Hits*. Dedicated music channels also emerged, playing an eclectic mix of styles and genres in rotation. Some videos were polished, but there was still room for low-budget creativity. MuchMusic and MusiquePlus presented videos, hosted special performances, and encouraged viewer participation.

"VIDEO DIDN'T KILL THE RADIO STARS: IT CREATED THEM EN MASSE."

— From *Have Not Been the Same: The CanRock Renaissance 1985–1995*

The Pursuit of Happiness

Front: Moe Berg. Back (left to right): Johnny Sinclair, Kris Abbott, Dave Gilby and Leslie Stanwyck.

Lead singer Moe Berg wore this pink denim jacket in several music videos, including "She's So Young," "Killed by Love," and "I'm an Adult Now."

The Pursuit of Happiness formed in Toronto in the 1980s. Innovative and independent, they self-produced their first music video, "I'm an Adult Now," on a shoestring budget. With airplay on MuchMusic, the song became a hit even before its release on cassette or vinyl. The band showed that they could make it on their own terms, helping to pave the way for an explosion of innovative Canadian indie artists.

Leonard Cohen
1965

Spotlight on Lyrics

THROUGH HONEST POETIC LANGUAGE, *CHANSONNIERS* AND SINGER-SONGWRITERS MADE POPULAR MUSIC MORE PERSONAL.

Quebec's *chansonniers* are celebrated for their poetic depictions of people, places and experiences that fostered a unique sense of identity. In English Canada, singer-songwriters shared personal experiences, relationships, and social commentary. All of these artists were voices of social, cultural and political significance.

Esquire

Murray McLauchlan

Murray McLauchlan began playing Toronto's Yorkville coffee houses as a teenager in the mid-1960s. His free spirit, captured in his music, reflected the bohemian lifestyle associated with this scene. Drawing upon stories of daily life, class struggle, and social justice, McLauchlan's music combines folk, country, rock and pop sensibilities.

McLauchlan used this guitar case as he hitchhiked and hopped freight trains across Canada in 1965. It was built for him by Nick Hapanovitch, a friend from art school.

Robert Charlebois performing in Paris, France
November 1973

Robert Charlebois

Robert Charlebois' early music was closely linked to the *chansonnier* style of the 1950s and '60s. By the late 1960s, he was rocking the boat in ways that had a profound impact on popular music in Quebec. He "went electric," and drew upon popular language — incorporating profanity, *joual*, and Québécois expressions in his lyrics.

Some of Charlebois' best-known works are collaborations with artists such as Mouffe, Réjean Ducharme, Claude Péloquin and Louise Forestier. His inventive approach to sound and musicality remains influential to this day.

↑

Joni Mitchell at
Sunset Sound recording studio
Los Angeles, California
1967

Joni Mitchell

Joni Mitchell emerged as a folk virtuoso in the 1960s. Known for her intricate guitar work, poetic songwriting, and vocal abilities, she continued to develop and experiment in the years that followed. Candidly voicing her inner worlds and personal experiences, Mitchell's lyrics address wide-ranging themes including the passage of time, social issues, love, and loss.

Blue, released in 1971, is considered one of the first confessional singer-songwriter albums. Mitchell's profound artistry continues to resonate with musicians and listeners.

Kate and Anna McGarrigle

Kate and Anna McGarrigle were born in Montréal, and grew up in the village of Saint-Sauveur-des-Monts, Quebec. The sisters freely blended folk traditions from English and French Canada with those of the United States.

Playing multiple instruments, they incorporated guitar, piano, accordion and banjo into their music. They brought their own experiences and creative voices into their work through evocative lyrics and remarkable vocal harmonies.

← The McGarrigles learned their first chords on this Gibson Archtop guitar. Dating from the 1920s, its body is marked with the names of friends and favourite artists.

CHAPTER 3

POPULAR MUSIC IS... POLITICAL

Artists and audiences are active. Through music, they question, engage, provoke and protest. They challenge the status quo and ignite change.

Vietnam War protesters on Granville Street in Vancouver, British Columbia
October 1970

all U.S. TROOPS from Vietnam NOW!
Withdraw all U.S. TROOPS from Vietnam NOW!
Vietnam for the Vietnamese
Vietnam for the Vietnamese
from Vietnam NOW

Rock promoter Ritchie Yorke during the Maple Music Junket. This event brought roughly 100 European journalists to Canada for a multi-city music showcase in 1972.

Turning Up the Volume

CANADA'S MUSIC INDUSTRY OWES MUCH TO GRASSROOTS ENGAGEMENT.

For years, Canadian artists had to make it big internationally before attracting much attention at home — but change was in the air. Through the 1960s and '70s, activists pushed to build greater exposure for Canadian musicians. This included increased radio play, and the beginnings of a Canadian star system.

Rock Nationalism in English Canada

The push to recognize Canadian talent gained momentum in the 1960s, notably through rock journalists at *RPM* magazine. In addition to its edgy editorials and cartoons, *RPM* introduced Canada's first national music chart.

Frustrated by the relative lack of Canadian music on the airwaves, *RPM* created a buzz around homegrown talent, advocated for increased Canadian content on the radio, and sought to assert Canada's cultural relevance on the world stage.

Controlling the Airwaves

INCREASING CANADIAN CONTENT OR "CANCON" ON THE RADIO WAS A STRATEGY TO SUPPORT THE INDUSTRY'S GROWTH — BUT NOT EVERYONE AGREED WITH THIS APPROACH.

Some artists saw value in the strategy, while others feared it might suggest that they hadn't made it on their own. Many commercial broadcasters, in turn, argued that Canada didn't have enough domestic talent to keep the airwaves fresh. In the end, the federal government chose to regulate Canadian content, believing that supporting popular artists positioned Canada as a modern, unified nation.

RPM co-founder Walt Grealis wearing the magazine's beaver mascot costume ↑

Crowbar

Hamilton-area band Crowbar formed around 1970, after playing back-up for influential bandleader Ronnie Hawkins. They released "Oh, What a Feeling" on January 18, 1971 — the same day that CanCon went into effect. The song quickly climbed the charts and is widely considered the first CanCon hit.

Crowbar lived in a manor house that they called "Bad Manors." Ancaster, Ontario
Around 1971

↰

As a playful promotional tactic, Daffodil Records included actual crowbars in their press kits for Crowbar's *Bad Manors* album.

Creating a National Awards System

k.d. lang accepting her first JUNO Award
1985

THE *RPM* GOLD LEAF AWARDS, LAUNCHED IN 1964, WERE CANADA'S FIRST NATIONAL MUSIC AWARDS.

RPM magazine's goal was to establish a recognition system for artists across Canada. The Gold Leaf Awards gained momentum. In 1971 they were renamed the JUNO Awards — a nod to Pierre Juneau, a powerful advocate for CanCon regulations. The ceremony has been televised across Canada since 1975.

Expanding the Spotlight

Diane Tell accepting a Prix Félix
October 1981

As Canada's music industry took shape, the spotlight did not shine equally on all artists. Language, race, gender and genre were common barriers to mainstream exposure. Many took action to expand representation in the industry.

Winston "Boyo" Hammond and Dan Hill at the Canadian Black Music Awards ceremony
March 1985

1979: The Prix Félix were established to recognize Quebec music, which already had its own distinct star system and fan base.

1981: The U-Knows, later renamed the CASBYs, recognized independent and alternative artists.

1984: The Black Music Association of Canada hosted awards ceremonies, and lobbied for the inclusion of music from the African diaspora at the JUNOs.

This momentum carried into the 1990s. The Canadian Aboriginal Music Awards were established in 1999, becoming the Indigenous Music Awards in 2015.

Manitoba Centennial Pop Festival
1970

Challenging Canada

THROUGH THEIR MUSIC, ARTISTS RESISTED THE IDEA OF A SINGLE CANADIAN IDENTITY.

During this period of upheaval, students, activists, and thought leaders became involved in global movements for liberation and equality. They questioned what "Canada" was all about. Many francophone, Indigenous, and Black artists expressed alternate visions of cultural identity and nationhood through their music.

Being Québécois

IN MUSIC, AS IN POLITICS, MANY QUÉBÉCOIS ARTISTS CONTESTED THE IDEA THAT THEY WERE PART OF A BROADER CANADIAN NATION.

Many Québécois musicians promoted and celebrated their linguistic and cultural distinctiveness. They stressed the importance of telling their own stories in their own language. Musicians often took part in growing nationalist movements, calling out challenges posed by Canada's anglophone majority, while celebrating Quebec's uniqueness.

Pauline Julien

Pauline Julien was a singer, actress, and political activist. An advocate for Quebec independence and women's rights, she is well known for her influential recording of the song "Mommy."

Written by Gilles Richer and Marc Gélinas, the song revolves around a child in the future. Addressing her mother, the child describes a Quebec in which the only remaining traces of her francophone culture are the names of streets, towns and people.

Pauline Julien on stage at the Théâtre du Nouveau Monde Montréal, Quebec
September 1975

1 fois 5

The show *1 fois 5* was the highlight of Saint-Jean-Baptiste festivities in Montréal and Québec City in 1976. Five celebrated artists shared the stage. Political and poetic, the performances fostered a sense of shared Québécois identity. An album was recorded at the Montréal show on Mount Royal, with more than 300,000 people in attendance.

Left to right:
Claude Léveillée, Yvon Deschamps, Jean-Pierre Ferland, Gilles Vigneault and Robert Charlebois
1976

Indigenous Expressions

INDIGENOUS ARTISTS CHALLENGED THE IDEA OF CANADA ITSELF.

By the 1960s, Indigenous Peoples had faced centuries of restrictive measures, and many children had been sent to residential schools. The "Sixties Scoop" was also underway, when large numbers of Indigenous children were forcibly removed from their communities.

Indigenous artists claimed space by sharing their experiences and perspectives. Some celebrated language and cultural vitality through song. Others were more direct, calling out racism and state aggression.

Alanis Obomsawin

Acclaimed filmmaker Alanis Obomsawin began her career as a singer. Her work confronts discrimination, systemic oppression, colonization, and violence against women.

Singing in Abenaki, English, and French, Obomsawin was influenced by the history, songs and stories that she learned from family on the reserve. Her music is also shaped by her youth in the predominantly white community of Trois-Rivières, Quebec.

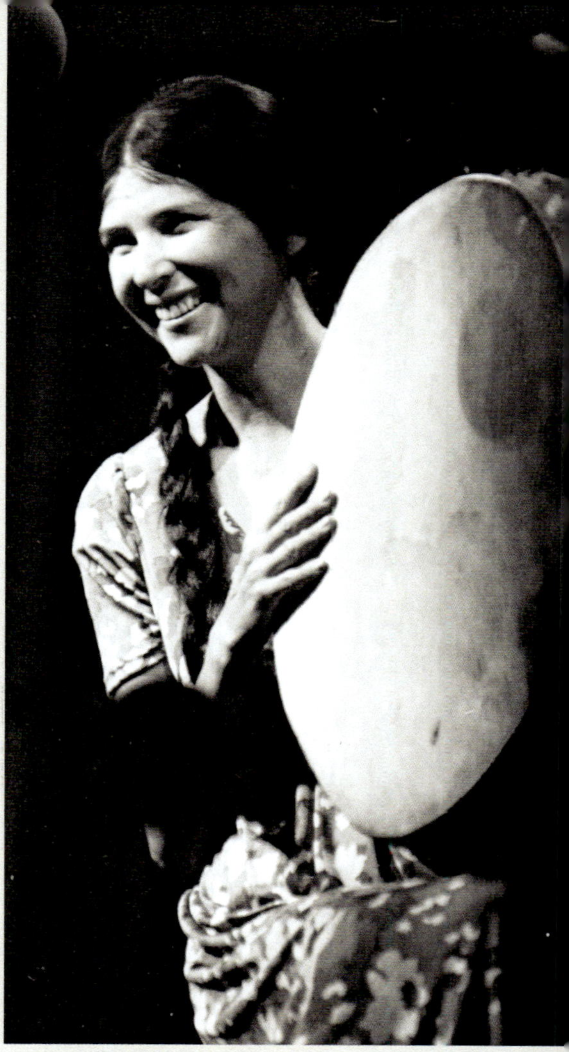

Alanis Obomsawin
at the Mariposa Folk Festival
Toronto, Ontario
1970

"I PITY THE COUNTRY, I PITY THE STATE AND THE MIND OF A MAN, WHO THRIVES ON HATE."

— Lyrics from "I Pity the Country" by Willie Dunn, a musician and filmmaker of Mi'kmaw and Scottish descent

Ray St. Germain performed in this leather jacket during the 1980s.

Ray St. Germain

Dubbed "Winnipeg's Elvis," Ray St. Germain was a Métis musician, radio DJ, television presenter, and producer. In the 1960s, he hosted CBC's *Hootenanny*, a youth-focused television show. He went on to spend 13 years with the variety series *Big Sky Country*.

St. Germain recorded "The Métis" in the late 1970s. It is one of his most popular songs, telling the story of Louis Riel and the Battle of Batoche. St. Germain received the Aboriginal Order of Canada in 1985.

Black Artists Break New Ground

BLACK ARTISTS HAVE BEEN UNDER-REPRESENTED IN CANADA FOR DECADES.

Vibrant communities embraced genres such as R&B and hip hop, but this music enjoyed little mainstream radio play or visibility in Canada. Black artists challenged the status quo, demanding that the industry become more representative of Canada's diverse population.

Break Dance '84
Poster

↳

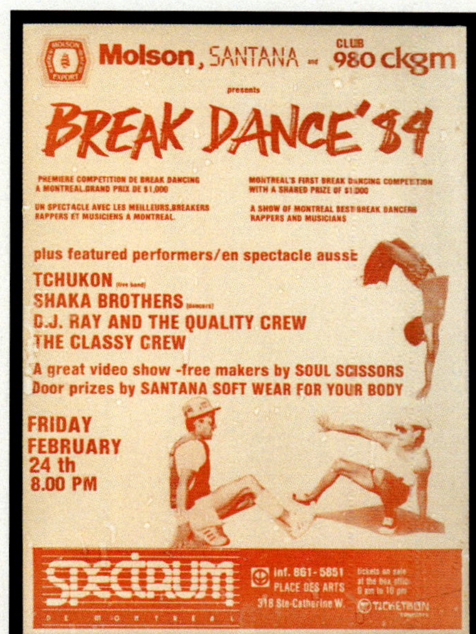

Break Dance '84

Break Dance '84 was held at the Spectrum de Montréal. Bringing together dancers, rappers, and other musicians, it received strong media coverage, raising the profile of hip hop in Quebec.

Originally planned as a single show, Break Dance '84 grew to include 13 sold-out performances. The event was hosted by DJ Michael Williams. His radio show, *Club 980*, was an important platform for music in Montréal. Williams went on to VJ shows such as *Rap City* and *Soul in the City* on MuchMusic.

Michie Mee (right) and DJ L.A. Luv
1989

Michie Mee wore this stage clothing, designed by style icon Dapper Dan, during the late 1980s.

↳

Michie Mee

Michie Mee was the first Canadian hip hop artist signed to a U.S. record label. With Jamaican roots, and experience in the Toronto and New York scenes, she incorporated elements of dancehall and reggae — along with Canadian references — into her music.

Michie Mee was a powerful performer at rap battles, and brought this same creativity to her look. Her compelling voice shaped Canada's hip hop scene, while asserting its presence and validity.

The Northern Pikes, left to right: Glen Hollingshead, Jay Semko, Bryan Potvin and Merl Bryck

June 1984

Challenging Convention

INCREASINGLY, AND IN NEW WAYS, ARTISTS POLITICIZED MUSIC WHILE CASTING A CRITICAL EYE OVER THE POPULAR MUSIC LANDSCAPE.

As Canada's music industry expanded in the late 1970s and the '80s, many artists grew increasingly disillusioned. Through new genres and approaches, they challenged artistic and social norms, critiqued contemporary culture, and rebelled against authority and conformity. Underground music systems fuelled alternative sounds and scenes.

Against the Grain

DURING THE LATE 1970s AND THE '80s, SOME ARTISTS REJECTED SO-CALLED MAINSTREAM CULTURE, PUSHING BACK AGAINST CONFORMITY.

Metal bands brought jarring new sounds and themes into the popular music sphere. New genres, such as punk, challenged social norms and reflected a backlash against the mainstream music industry. Artists also transformed existing genres, such as opera and performance art, presenting conventional forms in new ways.

Voïvod

Voïvod is a heavy metal band with an eclectic style from Jonquière, Quebec. Formed in 1982, they brought metal and progressive rock together in albums such as *Dimension Hatröss* and *Nothingface*.

Their lyrics explore science fiction, the Cold War, and post-apocalyptic themes, while their music is marked by dissonant chords and abrupt changes in rhythm. Voïvod continues to subvert norms in the metal world, prioritizing creative freedom in their art.

← Voïvod's lead singer, Denis Bélanger, wore this stage gear while performing in the 1980s.

The Dishrags

The Dishrags were one of the first all-female punk bands in North America. They started as teens in Saanich, British Columbia, in the late 1970s. They soon moved to Vancouver, becoming part of a mutually supportive fringe punk community.

All-female punk bands were rare. The Dishrags resisted pressure to sexualize their image, focusing instead on their art. By 1979, they were opening for big international acts such as The Clash and Bo Diddley.

Jade Blade bought this Marlin electric guitar as a teenager in 1976. She played it when The Dishrags took part in what is widely considered Vancouver's first punk show in 1977.

Left to right:
Scout, Jade Blade
and Dale Powers
June 1978

Indie and Alternative Music

INDIE AND ALTERNATIVE MUSICIANS ASSERTED THEIR INDEPENDENCE AND PLAYED BY THEIR OWN RULES.

Rock bands in the 1980s were often encouraged to follow a mainstream path, conforming to trends and performing cover songs until they were recognized. Indie artists rejected this system. Less concerned with commercial success, they prioritized creative autonomy and were patient in finding their audiences.

The Northern Pikes

Formed in 1984, indie rockers The Northern Pikes forged their own route through original songwriting, independent recording, and creative self-promotion. They were popular on college radio, releasing two independent albums before signing with Virgin Records in 1986. The Pikes soon gained mainstream attention with hits such as "Teenland," "She Ain't Pretty," and "Things I Do for Money."

Bryan Potvin used this Yamaha LSX-21 acoustic guitar to write, warm up, record, and tour. He wrote the song "She Ain't Pretty" ← with this guitar.

The Grapes of Wrath

The Grapes of Wrath formed in 1983. The band's founding members met as teenagers in Kelowna, British Columbia. They experimented with home movies and punk-rock influences, and ignored advice to play more covers. Their first full-length album, *September Bowl of Green*, was popular on alternative radio and MuchMusic. An international breakthrough soon followed with *Now and Again*. The band achieved mainstream success while maintaining its creative independence.

↰

Poster for a 1988 concert featuring The Grapes of Wrath with guest Sarah McLachlan in Vancouver, British Columbia

Brian Wright-McLeod →
in the studio
1987

Alternative Airwaves

INDEPENDENT RADIO HELPED SHAPE VIBRANT UNDERGROUND MUSIC SCENES.

Curious listeners, seeking new sounds, eagerly explored independent radio. Alternative artists, in turn, found their audiences through college, university, and community stations, as well as late-night programs such as CBC Radio's *Brave New Waves* and *Night Lines*.

Renegade Radio

Renegade Radio was a live weekly program devoted to Indigenous music and issues. It aired on CKLN-FM, the campus radio station at Ryerson (now Toronto Metropolitan) University. The show was hosted by Brian Wright-McLeod from 1983 until 2011. Wright-McLeod, who is Dakota and Anishinabe, is a noted journalist, producer, writer, artist and educator.

Renegade Radio "Original Landlord" promotional shirt, designed by host Brian Wright-McLeod. The back reads, "Is That A Treaty In Your Pocket? Or Are You Just Glad To See Me!"

Spotlight on Protest

SOCIAL AND POLITICAL ISSUES, FROM INEQUALITY TO THE ENVIRONMENT, WERE TOP OF MIND IN THE '60s, '70s AND '80s.

Artists in Canada harnessed the power of popular music to communicate complex ideas in accessible ways. Responding directly to contemporary issues, musicians inspired audiences to think deeply and differently about the world around them.

Women's Liberation rally in Toronto
1970

Give Peace a Chance

In 1969, John Lennon and Yoko Ono staged a week-long "Bed-In for Peace" at the Queen Elizabeth Hotel in Montréal. Many joined them, including musicians, activists, religious figures, and politicians. From their hotel room, they recorded the iconic song "Give Peace a Chance." The Bed-In furthered Canada's reputation as both a peace-loving country and a refuge for American draft-dodgers.

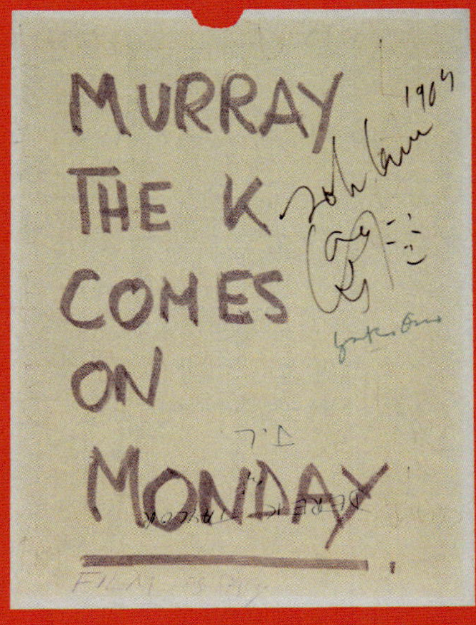

This piece of paper was taped to the wall of John and Yoko's hotel room at the Montréal Bed-In. It includes doodles of them, along with their signatures. "Murray the K" Kaufman was a well-known DJ and early supporter of The Beatles.

The Parachute Club

The Parachute Club was part of Toronto's active Queen Street West scene. They engaged with social and political issues connected to race, gender, sexual equality, and peace in their art. The band's hit "Rise Up" was an anthem of empowerment in the 1980s, celebrating equity and inclusion. "Rise Up" was performed at Toronto Pride soon after its release.

Lorraine Segato and Margo Davidson
1985

↑

Lorraine Segato played this 1982 Fender Telecaster electric guitar as a solo artist, and with groups including V, Mama Quilla II, and The Parachute Club. It appears in the music video for "Rise Up."

Truths & Rights

Truths & Rights is one of Canada's earliest reggae acts. They had a significant impact on music scenes in and beyond Toronto in the late 1970s and early '80s. The group incorporated musical elements from many sources, reflecting band members' roots in Trinidad, Guyana, the Eastern Caribbean, and Nova Scotia.

Truths & Rights' lyrics address Canadian social and political issues. A good example is their first single, "Acid Rain," which names a prevailing environmental concern of the 1980s.

Truths & Rights "Acid Rain" Single
1980

Ongoing Waves of Influence

The energy of popular music from the '60s, '70s and '80s doesn't end in 1989. These songs continue to draw audiences, move listeners, and spark change. They also impact new music, through influence and reaction, in a dynamic ongoing process. Popular music keeps emerging, forming and reforming. What resonates today is always connected to what has come before.

So Much to Explore

ROCK, HIP HOP, FOLK, NEW WAVE — AND EVERYTHING IN BETWEEN.

The ’60s, ’70s and ’80s were marked by a wide variety of unforgettable songs, artists and genres. The following playlist provides a starting point to begin exploring the breadth of popular music in Canada.

Lillian Allen, “I Fight Back,” 1986
April Wine, “Just Between You and Me,” 1981
Bachman-Turner Overdrive, “Takin’ Care of Business,” 1973
The Band, “The Weight,” 1968
Beau Dommage, “Tous les palmiers,” 1974
Salome Bey, “Hit the Nail Right on the Head,” 1970
Blue Rodeo, “Try,” 1987
CANO, “Au nord de notre vie,” 1980
César et les Romains, “Splish Splash,” 1965
Robert Charlebois and Louise Forestier, “Lindberg,” 1968
Chilliwack, “My Girl (Gone Gone Gone),” 1981
Bruce Cockburn, “If I Had a Rocket Launcher,” 1984
Leonard Cohen, “Suzanne,” 1968
The Collectors, “What Love Suite,” 1968
The Cougars, “I Wish It Would Rain,” 1970
Crosby, Stills, Nash & Young, “Ohio,” 1970

Crowbar, "Oh, What a Feeling," 1971
Dance Appeal, "Can't Repress the Cause," 1991
Clémence DesRochers, "La vie d'factrie," 1962
Céline Dion, "Ne partez pas sans moi," 1988
The Dishrags, "Past Is Past," 1979
Figgy Duff, "Weather Out the Storm," 1990
Diane Dufresne, "Tiens-toé ben j'arrive," 1972
Willie Dunn, "I Pity the Country," 1972
Jean-Pierre Ferland, "God Is an American," 1970
FM, "Up to You," 1980
Glass Tiger, "Don't Forget Me (When I'm Gone)," 1986
The Grapes of Wrath, "All the Things I Wasn't," 1989
The Guess Who, "American Woman," 1970
Harmonium, "Depuis l'automne," 1975
The Headpins, "Don't It Make Ya Feel," 1982
Ian & Sylvia, "Four Strong Winds," 1963
Terry Jacks, "Seasons in the Sun," 1973
The Jeff Healey Band, "Angel Eyes," 1988
Pauline Julien, "Mommy," 1974
Kashtin, "E Uassiuian" (My Childhood), 1989
Pierre Lalonde, "Donne-moi ta bouche," 1968
Daniel Lavoie, "Ils s'aiment," 1983
Jacqueline Lemay, "La moitié du monde est une femme," 1975
Gordon Lightfoot, "If You Could Read My Mind," 1970

Lighthouse, “One Fine Morning,” 1971
Maestro Fresh Wes, “Let Your Backbone Slide,” 1990
Rita MacNeil, “Born a Woman,” 1975
Marjo, “Chats sauvages,” 1986
Martha and the Muffins, “Echo Beach,” 1980
Kate and Anna McGarrigle, “Heart Like a Wheel,” 1975
Sarah McLachlan, “Vox,” 1988
Murray McLauchlan, “Child’s Song,” 1971
Michie Mee and L.A. Luv, “Elements of Style,” 1987
Joni Mitchell, “Both Sides, Now,” 1969
Willy Mitchell, “Call of the Moose,” 1980
Mitsou, “Bye bye mon cowboy,” 1988
Anne Murray, “Snowbird,” 1970
Alannah Myles, “Black Velvet,” 1989
The Nylons, “Kiss Him Goodbye,” 1987
Alanis Obomsawin, “Bush Lady,” 1985
Octobre, “La maudite machine,” 1972
Offenbach, “Câline de blues,” 1972
Mary Margaret O’Hara, “Year in Song,” 1988
The Parachute Club, “Rise Up,” 1983
Payola$, “Eyes of a Stranger,” 1982
Pierre Perpall, “We Can Make It,” 1984
Paul Piché, “L’escalier,” 1980
The Plastic Ono Band, “Give Peace a Chance,” 1969

Ginette Reno, "Je ne suis qu'une chanson," 1979
Michèle Richard, "Les boîtes à gogo," 1966
Rough Trade, "High School Confidential," 1980
Rush, "Limelight," 1981
Jackie Shane, "Any Other Way," 1963
Shingoose, "Silver River," 1975
Jane Siberry, "One More Colour," 1985
The Squires, "Aurora," 1963
Martine St-Clair, "Ce soir, l'amour est dans tes yeux," 1986
Steppenwolf, "Born to Be Wild," 1968
Ray St. Germain, "The Métis," around 1978
Sugluk, "Fall Away," 1975
Vicky Taylor, "Birth Control Blues," 1965
Diane Tell, "Si j'étais un homme," 1980
Willie Thrasher, "Spirit Child," 1980
Toulouse, "Funkysation," 1979
The Tragically Hip, "New Orleans Is Sinking," 1989
Trooper, "Raise a Little Hell," 1978
Truths & Rights, "Acid Rain," 1980
Gilles Vigneault, "Mon pays," 1965
Gino Vannelli, "I Just Wanna Stop," 1978
Roch Voisine, "Hélène," 1989
Nanette Workman, "Lady Marmalade," 1975
Neil Young and Crazy Horse, "Hey Hey, My My (Into the Black)," 1979

Contributions

Retro – Popular Music in Canada From the '60s, '70s and '80s would not have been possible without the contributions and support of our colleagues at the Canadian Museum of History. In particular, we would like to thank members of the exhibition core team: Louis-Antoine Blanchette, Stefanie Brantner, Colin Chen, Carolyn Lecorre, Guillaume Lord, Rachel Locatelli, Julie Savard, Léonie Théberge and Jimmy Youssef.

We also extend our warm thanks to the many colleagues and collaborators who contributed their expertise to this project: Mayusha Aubin, Nancy Bacon, Chantal Baril, Meagan Barnhart, Laurence Beaumier-Breton, Ellen Bertrand, Kenn Bingley, Britt Braaten, Stéphane Breton, Claire Champ, Brenna Cook, Marquis Côté, Steven Darby, Danielle Dezort, Caroline Dromaguet, Nicolas Duval, David Fingland, Bianca Gendreau, Pierre Girard, Lorraine Gouin, Amanda Gould, Julie Guinard, Brigitte Hamon, Meghan Jennings, Jessica Lafrance-Hwang, Gar Lam, Rebecca Latourell, Julie Leclair, Hans Levac, Emily Lin, Katia Macias-Valadez, Sylvia Mauro, Jasmine McMorran, Jennifer Ann Mills, Yasmine Mingay, Cathy Mitchell, Shannon Mooney, Glenn Ogden, Eric Pallotta, Jem Pellerin, Caitlyn Picard, Mika Posen, Christine Quinn, Patrice Rémillard, Dominique Savard, Laura Sanchini, Martine Seewaldt, Jessica Shaw, Alison Smith-Welsh, Annie Tanguay, Dominique Taylor, Veronique Thiffault, James Whitham, Erin Wilson and Nathan Wisnicki.

Our advisory committee provided valuable insight throughout the project. A heartfelt thank you to Sandria P. Bouliane, Rob Bowman, William Echard, Charity Marsh, Michael Williams and Brian Wright-McLeod for their expertise and engagement.

A sincere thank you to the many artists who have graciously donated instruments, stage clothing, and other meaningful items to the Museum during the development of this project. Thank you as well to the musicians and organizations that loaned treasures to us, or helped to make these loans possible. Your contributions have been crucial in making this exhibition a success.

Finally, we would like to thank Jenny Ellison, Chelsea Osmond and Pascal Scallon-Chouinard for the production of this book.

Photo Credits

p. 8–9 Photo: Boris Spremo, *Toronto Star* via Getty Images

p. 10–11 CTV / Bell Media Inc.

p. 14 Photo: CMH IMG2024-026-0008-Dm | Object: Canadian Museum of History, 2020.204.5, Michèle Richard Collection

p. 15 Photo: Pierre McCann, BAnQ, *La Presse* fonds P833,S2,D4593,P20

p. 17 Photo: CMH IMG2024-0266-0062-Dm | Objects: Canadian Museum of History, 2015.39.1.1-5, Denis L'Espérance Collection

p. 18–19 Photo: Barney Charach, John Einarson Collection

p. 19 Photo: CMH IMG2024-0266-0044-Dm | Object: Canadian Museum of History, 3927.1

p. 20 (Left) Courtesy of Jay Douglas

p. 20 (Right) Photos: CMH IMG2024-0266-0056-Dm, IMG2024-0266-0057-Dm | Objects: Canadian Museum of History, 2021.23.1-2

p. 21 (Top) Michael Ochs Archives via Getty Images

p. 21 (Bottom) Photo: CMH IMG2016-0172-0003-Dm | Object: Canadian Museum of History, 95-32.1, Randy Bachman Collection

p. 22–23 Photo: Dale Brazao, *Toronto Star* via Getty Images

p. 24 Courtesy of Canada Lands

p. 25 Photo: Pierre Perpall; CMH IMG2024-0064-0025-Dm

p. 26–27 Photo: Fin Costello / Redferns via Getty Images

p. 28–29 Photo: CMH IMG2024-0266-0052-Dm | Objects: Canadian Museum of History, 2001.122.2.1, 2001.122.3.1, 2001.122.6.5, Rush Collection

p. 30 Photo: Robert Nadon, BAnQ, *La Presse* fonds 06M,P833,S2,D1724,P5

p. 31 (Left) Photo: Dee Lippingwell

p. 31 (Right) Photo: CMH IMG2024-026-0002-Dm | Objects: Canadian Museum of History, 2010.221.41.1-2, Ra McGuire Trooper Collection

p. 32–33 Photo: Dick Darrell, *Toronto Star* via Getty Images

p. 34 Photo: CMH IMG2024-026-0001-Dm | Objects: Canadian Museum of History, 3899.1-18, Basil Philistin Record Sleeve Collection

p. 36 Photo: Independent News and Media via Getty Images

p. 37 (Left) Photo: CMH IMG2024-0266-0062-Dm | Objects: Canadian Museum of History, 2018.299.1.1-2, Gift of Anne Murray

p. 37 (Right) Photo: Bill Langstroth

p. 38–39 Photo: John Scheele

p. 40 Photo: CMH IMG2024-0266-0048-Dm | Loan: Courtesy of the Estate of Robbie Robertson

p. 41 (Top) Photo: CMH IMG2024-0266-0047-Dm | Loan: Courtesy of Michel Normandeau

p. 41 (Bottom) Courtesy of Michel Normandeau

p. 43 Photo: David Davies, York University Libraries, *Toronto Telegram* fonds ASC03490

p. 44 Photo: Reg Innell, *Toronto Star* via Getty Images

p. 47 (Top) Photo: CMH IMG2024-0266-0034-Dm | Objects: Canadian Museum of History, 2006.41.1-3 a-b

p. 47 (Bottom) Photo: CMH IMG2024-026-0022-Dm | Loans: Ingenium 1987.0073.001; Courtesy of Elizabeth Logue

p. 49 Photo: Reg Innell, *Toronto Star* via Getty Images

p. 50 Photo: Jorge Zontal, True North Records

p. 51 Photo: Jean-Yves Létourneau, BAnQ, *La Presse* fonds P833,S5,D1989-0364,P1

p. 52 Photo: Jean Blais

p. 53 MUCH, Bell Media

p. 54 Book citation: Michael Barclay, Ian A.D. Jack, and Jason Schneider, *Have Not Been the Same: The Can Rock Renaissance 1985–1995*, rev. ed. (Toronto: ECW Press, 2011), p. 26

p. 55 (Left) Photo: CMH IMG2024-026-0010-Dm | Object: Canadian Museum of History, 2022.118.1, Gift of Moe Berg

p. 55 (Right) Photo: Bernard Weil *Toronto Star* via Getty Images

p. 56–57 *Ladies and Gentlemen . . . Mr. Leonard Cohen*, 1965, NFB

p. 58 Photo: CMH IMG2024-0266-0040-Dm | Object: Canadian Museum of History, 2020.147.1, Murray McLauchlan Collection

p. 59 Photo: Michel Artault, Gamma-Rapho via Getty Images

p. 60 Photo: Sulfiati Magnuson, Michael Ochs Archives via Getty Images

p. 61 Photo: CMH IMG2024-0266-0050-Dm | Loan: Courtesy of the McGarrigle Family

p. 63 Photo: Glenn Baglo, *Vancouver Sun*, a division of Postmedia Network Inc.

p. 64 Photo: Ron Bull, *Toronto Star* via Getty Images

p. 67 Courtesy of the Stan Klees Estate

p. 68 Photo: CMH IMG-2024-0266-0036-Dm | Object: Canadian Museum of History, 2016.28.1, Frank Davies Collection

p. 68–69 Photo: Annette Yorke, Ritchie Yorke Archives

p. 70 Photo: Boris Spremo, *Toronto Star* via Getty Images

p. 71 (Top) Photo: Pierre Côté, BAnQ, *La Presse* fonds P833,S2,D5174,P3

p. 71 (Bottom) Photo: Colin McConnell, *Toronto Star* via Getty Images

p. 72 Photo: Gerry Kopelow

p. 75 Photo: Bernard Georges

p. 76–77 Photo: René Picard, BAnQ, *La Presse* fonds, P833,S4,D785,P69

p. 79 Photo: Norm Betts, York University Libraries, *Toronto Telegram* fonds ASC17401

p. 81 Photo: CMH IMG2024-0266-0042-Dm | Object: Canadian Museum of History, 2024.44.1, Ray St. Germain Collection

p. 83 Photo: CMH IMG2024-0266-0049-Dm | Loan: Courtesy of Eugene Poku

p. 84 Photo: Al Pereira, Michael Ochs Archives via Getty Images

p. 85 Photo: CMH IMG2024-0266-0061-Dm | Loan: Courtesy of Michie Mee (Michelle McCullock)

p. 86 Photo: Grant Kernan

p. 89 Photo: CMH IMG2024-0266-0063-Dm | Loan: Courtesy of Michel Langevin and Denis Bélanger

p. 90 Photo: CMH IMG2024-0266-0037-Dm | Object: Canadian Museum of History, 2020.109.1, The Dishrags Collection, Gift of Jill Bain

p. 91 Photo: Don Denton

p. 93 Photo: CMH IMG2024-0266-0038-Dm | Object: Canadian Museum of History, 2020.138.1, Bryan Potvin Collection

p. 95 Photo: CMH IMG2024-026-0013-Dm | Object: Canadian Museum of History, 2021-F0007.5, The Grapes of Wrath Collection, Gift of Chris Hooper

p. 96–97 Photo: Andrew Bainbridge, courtesy of Brian Wright-McLeod

p. 97 Photo: CMH IMG2024-0266-0054-Dm | Object: Canadian Museum of History, 2021.59.1, Brian Wright-McLeod Collection

p. 98–99 Photo: Reg Innell, *Toronto Star* via Getty Images

p. 100 © Yoko Ono Lennon. Photo: CMH IMG2024-026-0003-Dm | Object: Canadian Museum of History, 2015.83.1

p. 101 (Left) Photo: Ken Faught, *Toronto Star* via Getty Images

p. 101 (Right) Photo: CMH IMG2019-0066-0001-Dm | Object: Canadian Museum of History, 2017.74.1.2 a-b, Lorraine Segato Collection

p. 102 Sleeve design: Ato Seitu. Photo: CMH IMG2024-026-0018-Dm | Object: Canadian Museum of History, 2938.1-2